THE
BOOK
OF Bad
HABITS

THE
BOOK
OF Bad
HABITS

PATRICK REGAN

**Andrews McMeel
Publishing, LLC**

Kansas City

06 07 08 09 10 SDB 10 9 8 7 6 5 4 3

ISBN-13: 978-0-7407-6076-1
ISBN-10: 0-7407-6076-9

Library of Congress Control Number: 2006923247

www.andrewsmcmeel.com

Photo Credits
Annie Griffiths Belt/Corbis: 43; Antoine Gyori/Corbis Sygma: 47; Austrian
Archives/Corbis: 9; Bettmann/Corbis: 3, 7, 15, 21, 23, 25, 29, 37, 39, 45, 49,
51, 53, 57, 63; Corbis: 13; Ed Eckstein/Corbis: 27; Gary Houlder/Corbis: 55;
Hulton-Deutsch Collection/Corbis: 5, 11, 31, 33; Norbert Schaefer/Corbis: 65;
Owen Franken/Corbis: 17; Stone: 59; Time & Life Pictures: 19, 61;
The Image Bank: 41; Vittoriano Rastelli/Corbis: 35

For Sister Jeanine Salak,
a fun nun if ever was one

COME, PENSIVE NUN,
DEVOUT AND PURE, SOBER,
STEADFAST, AND DEMURE...

—John Milton

PENSIVE? SOBER? DEMURE? NOT THESE LADIES, JOHN.

Welcome to *The Book of Bad Habits,* where women in black shoot, smoke, box, dance, and engage in all kinds of otherwise unsanctified behavior. Have these swingin' sisters lost their religion? Nah, they're just nuns having fun. After all, all pray and no play makes for a very dull day.

Wheee! Celibacy is fun!

For the Sisters of St. Nicotine's,
every day was "Ash Wednesday."

"Remember ladies,
what happens in Vegas stays in Vegas."

Down at Saint Mary's, the claims of immaculate conception were getting a little hard to believe.

Sporting clever disguises and armed with their "Hose of Absolution," Sisters Clara and Beatrice battle evil as the Convent Crusaders.

Downloading MP3s: The Early Years

Trying out this season's hot new one-piece

"Ah, Caravaggio, Raphael, Leonardo . . .
I'd have dropped the habit for any one of them
in a Milan minute."

———

In a unanimous vote,

the Sisters of the Immaculate Heart of Mary

decided to cancel Sunday vespers and watch

Desperate Housewives instead.

Known around the neighborhood as the "Spying Nun," Sister Augustine was becoming a bit of a nuisance.

Support tougher nun laws!

The penguin habitat was always a favorite of zoo visitors.

Sisters Joan and Roberta belt out their singular version of Zeppelin's "Stairway to Heaven."

The original Hail Mary pass

Monsignor O'Reilly's chronic flatulence was becoming a serious problem.

Sister Josephine enjoys her turn as
Mr. Fenwick's hose-handling assistant.

Once again, Sister Martina was the odds-on favorite at the annual Woody Allen look-alike Ping-Pong tournament.

The "Bumpin' for Jesus" race was a highlight of the annual Sisters' Day Out.

Screw vespers—let's go fishin'!

Sister Jeanine was a little stung when

Sister Mildred beat her out for first chair,

but she had to admit, that bitch could blow.

Sister Mary Margaret reviews her audition tape for *Real World Vatican City.*

With her lightning-fast right and jackhammer left, Sister Theresa could lick any kid in the orphanage.

Inside the cloistered walls of St. Basil's,

if you needed a fix or a "favor,"

you talked to Sister Mary Jane.

Impure thoughts?

When it came to JFK,

Sister Celeste figured God would understand.

Sister Roberta goes yard at the annual

Nun & Sun summer picnic.

Outfitted in their winter camouflage, the sisters were known to attack from out of nowhere.

Equipped with the new HabitWing 3000, Sister Ramona was able to glide for miles.

"Hello, Sister. I love your outfit."

"Oh, haven't you heard?

White is the new black."

For the sisters of St. Agnes,

every day is judgment day.

"It's just the hair this time, Timmy.

But one more spit wad and he takes off an ear."

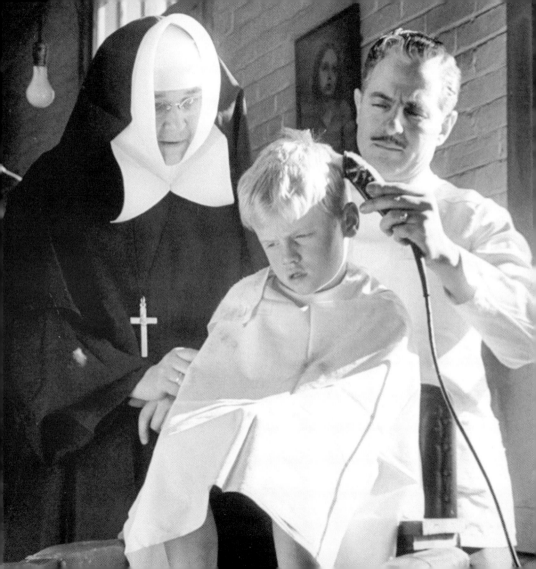

After downing a few green beers,
Sister Bridget and the boys get jiggy with it.

Bad habits die hard.

With grateful acknowledgment to my editor, Patty Rice, and to my parents, who footed the bill for ten years of Catholic education. A special thanks to the sisters of Our Lady of Perpetual Help grade school circa 1973 to 1978, who taught me to read and write. And this is the thanks you get. It's nothing personal. Honest.